EDitable

Stephanie Johnston

EDitable © 2022 Stephanie Johnston

All rights reserved.

No part of this publication may be reproduced, stored in a retrieval system, or transmitted, in any form or by any means, electronic, mechanical, photocopying, recording or otherwise, without the prior written permission of the presenters.

Stephanie Johnston asserts the moral right to be identified as author of this work.

Presentation by *BookLeaf Publishing*

Web: www.bookleafpub.com

E-mail: info@bookleafpub.com

ISBN: 9789357616997

First edition 2022

DEDICATION

I want to dedicate this book to everyone who has been a part of my recovery. I am so thankful for the army of people that stood beside me, and carried me when I felt I couldn't go any further. I especially want to dedicate this book to my recovery team and to the Bulimia Anorexia Nervosa Association (BANA). Jade, Nicole, Kim, Kia, Sarah, and Barb, I am so grateful for everything you helped me walk through. You have helped guide me down the path I am intended to live on and for that I am forever grateful!

PREFACE

All of these poems are from the heart. All of them are real things I was thinking during recovery. I don't share them for pity or sadness, but I share them to inspire others to keep going. Recovery is hard and I am still in recovery. Sharing this poetry is terrifying, but getting it out is something that helped me. If you are on your own recovery journey I encourage you to keep going, find a good support team, and know that you are worthy of recovery.

Sitting in Silence

I sit calmly in silence
But my brain is screaming
Like a growing fire
My thoughts consume me
A smile washes across my face
To hide the words that would replace
Yet I can't express them
Because it hurts to say them
For so long these words have been with me
They are now more realistic than positive
feelings
They happen every second
And any good thought
Is quickly replaced
What started as just one or two
Now is far too many to see any truth
In the mirror, when I look
I don't see me
I see a monster that no one should bother with
The reality is it hurts
Yet I can't unwind my brain
The cycle of shame continues another day
Because I hate myself
Which then I hate myself more
Until the hate is unbearable

I'm not proud of who I am
The perfect exterior for others
With struggles inside just for me
So yes I sit in silence
But that's to prevent more pain

Calculated

Everything is calculated
From time to eat
How much to eat
Where to eat
It feels safe
But also like I have no control
I try to go without
But my mind becomes a maze
Twists and turns
Leading to dead ends
Where words of failings exist
Constantly running to nowhere
Hoping to break free
But like a monster under the bed
The invisible fear grows
I don't want to always think
Always calculate my joy
Based on what I eat and when
I just want to enjoy a bite
Without calculating the risk
Yet when it comes down to it
Numbers are safe and real
ConstantI can go a day without
And simply cease the calculated risk

Never Enough

Too much or not enough
Control or loss
The constant battle of my brain
Every bite like a mountain
A steep mountain I must climb
The reward at the top far greater
But the bottom is uncomfortable
Every bit screams a thought
Dumb, ugly, stupid, failure
The thought of failure even worse
Letting everyone down
Confirming my flaws
Terrified the world will see the monster I am
The monster eating me from the inside out
Stealing every ounce of joy
But still hidden from the world
As the battle rages on
I seek control
To do things right
Because if I fall
I fear how long I will be down
I will always fight
But some days it feels easier to quit
Because do I deserve success
I don't know

Some days yes and some days no
So the battle rages on
The soldier growing tired each day

Overthinking

Like a virus
The mind is infiltrated
One suggestion at a time
Until nothing is your own
Joy stolen by thoughts
Thoughts of am I good enough
What did I look like
Will the photos be okay
I'm so fat and ugly
Sometimes wishing the words were more
profound
Not to increase the pain
But at least to justify intelligence
Simple words deserve simple solutions
Yet nothing is simple
The hours in my head
And in front of the mirror
Not for vanity
But to confirm what the enemy says
Never enough mentally or physically
Just dirt
To blow in the wind
And be passed by
Disappear to reappear

Fire Raging

Inside my world feels on fire
Every thought digs a deeper wound
No words escape
For so long silence was my protector
At the core I'm lost
Unsure of what I feel
Scared of the truth
That has been so easy to ignore
Shutting down and shutting out
So easy to do to to avoid the thoughts
Thoughts of being a burden
Fear of failure
Disappointing everyone
Losing what I know
The fire consumes
Until I find myself with tears streaming down
my face
In the quiet of solitude
The emotions are controlled once again
The fire rekindled
Waiting to spark until it consumes again
I don't want this reality
But it feels safe
So silence is where I sit
Because trying to explain

Just brings greater pain
No understanding of my own brain
So the fire rages on
Until the destruction is done

Who Am I

I know who I am
Yet I don't
How I act and what I love
That is my reality
Yet there is a part I hide
The part no one would like
The part raging with the voice of ED
The part that doesn't smile
The monstrous parts hidden so well
Tucked away from the world
For only me to hate
Now the fear
That as I heal
The inside will show on the outside
A monster no one could love
Too selfish to earn anyones care
Just a girl
Ugly inside and out
Scared I will lose everything
Disappoint everyone
Wanting to change, yet scared I wont
Scared I am a waste of time
Why do I get to get better
Feeling like I take up too much space
Some days I wish I could disappear

Disappear from others and ED
Find the real me
In amongst who I am and who I hide
Wanting change
But scared of what I will find

Funeral March

Silence all around
Lives keep moving
But here I stand
Knowing I'm working
But not how I want
I miss my old self
No thought of me
Comfortable in ignoring the pain
Yet I know I can't go back
Building a new me
To see the world differently
So why is that so scary
Me and ED
Two lives intertwined
To lose one would be a comfort
But also feel like a death
Death of something that served me well
Something that consumed my thoughts
And something that still does
I want to move in the sound of the world
Not the sound of ED

Fighting the Inevitable

The longer I fight
The harder the air I breathe
Every challenge harder
Until I lose me
Not sure who I am
And who I have hid for so long
The voice inside screaming
Yet no sound comes out
No sound, but intense pain
Pain that encloses like a blanket
So tightly wrapped
I loose feeling
I feel like parts of me are lost
So I cling to what I can
I know the parts I want
The parts that make me feel whole
The parts I love
The parts that fight
Yet I feel stuck
Sinking back until I'm lost
Scared that I can't do this
Scared I will let everyone down
Because that's why I fight
Not for me
I could care less

Because if I cared I would feel
Feelings shoved so deep that I'm scared
Scared to open up what I've numbed
Because numb protects
From falling to the bottom
Where all my pain and failings have fallen

Season 2

It's like the world is sped up
Yet I'm stuck watching the rerun
I can't imagine the finale
Even with hopes of more seasons
Waiting for the producer to quit
Yet time and time again the show goes on
Even when the main character is lost
No storyline to move them forward
And just annoying the audience
Hoping viewers keep watching
But waiting for it to all crash down
Lights, camera, stop
Yet the question of why remains
Why keep watching
Why do people care
Crumbling under expectation
The main character lost in the chaotic storyline
Wishing to close her eyes
Close her eyes and wake up from the nightmare
The nightmare of thoughts constantly swirling
Wishing for the mute button
But the TV stuck on stereo surround
Too loud to make out the words
But able to feel the pain of ringing ears
Wanting to get up and leave

But legs unwilling to move
Too tired from the fight
Too slow to get away
So the rerun plays
The main character lost each day
Background noise
Trying to get back

Recovery Road

I stand at the edge
A fork in the road
The gleaming comfort of fear
Or the unknown gaze of my life to be
I took the first step
Terrified as I saw the chasm below
But every step met with a new rung
Shaky at first
As the foundation grew
Rope and wood tied together
An incoherent mess
Met with patience
As the journey continues
And choices must be made
The difference made is clear
The new way starting to be paved
Although it is scary
Gratitude abounds
New rungs to be formed
With knowledge shared
So I walked alone
But found a way
Because you stood beside me
And helped pave my way
So I stand at the cross road

But the unknown gaze
Not as scary
Knowing each new rung
Inspired by time, in time
By you, with you
My path growing
With gratefulness for all of you

The Army

My mind is chaos
The world is calm
Everyone keeps moving
Even in their own trials
How did I get here
How did I fall
Just praying for peace
Peace I haven't felt since I was a kid
I long for my mind to quiet
Where I just do
Where I live my life for the kid I was
Where I live my life for me
No longer tied to what others think
Just joy in the here and now
Living in the moment
Rather than an observer of the story
One I never thought would be written
But one I'm beginning to understand
Even though it hurts
I grow in strength
On the days I break
I am held up by others
So my story remains
As one that is still being written
No clear ending

But clearly meant for something
Even if I can't see
Amongst the chaos of my mind
I fight
But never alone

The Reflection

Every time I look in the mirror
I don't recognize the reflection staring back
I see someone who is sick
Yet I see someone who is not sick enough
Wishing I just saw me
Yet every angle brings a new flaw
Brings a new loathing
Like eyes of daggers
My gaze pierces my heart
Until the reflection is a monster
And I just want to run
Run away from every thought
So that the pain I feel would end
Yet daily I feel like I walk through fire
Hoping I would find relief
Some days I do
Yet others feel like I'm the one holding the
match
Hands shaking
But hoping I don't make the flame worse
My chest crushed by fear
My lungs emptied by expectation
Yet I march on
Knowing this is not my ending
Knowing I want a different view

So for now I just don't see
But one day I hope I can
Hope I can look in the mirror
And see me
Just me

Two Lives

Two separate lives
One of reality
One to protect the reality of others
I don't want a secret
One that draws me to shame
Yet I cling to it
Making me weak
Yet strong
Strong in ability to hide
Yet hidden so well I disappear
The secret yelling to escape
Yet locked inside
To wind every fibre of my life
Into one giant knot
Each new strand
Trying to strangle
Strangle the act I put on
The one where I'm fine
The one where no one has to worry
The one where I'm normal
Wishing I could cut it loose
Set the secret free
Live one life
The life of imperfection
Yet of love

Two lives
Becoming one
The secret unwinding
To years of screaming and tears
But finally peace

Grateful

Grateful for the journey
The one that breaks me
The one that steals every last breath
I want to hide
Not to avoid pain
But just to get a break
Then I remember I'm grateful
Grateful for the friends and family that support
Grateful for my team
Grateful for every memory of fight
Grateful for the laughs, the tears
Grateful for every big and little cheer
When I wanted to stop
I was given more fight
Knowing my fight was given from God
Every word written by him
Every chapter grown with love
Every step one to share his grace
So some days I'm lost
But everyday I'm grateful
Grateful for what I've learned
When I'm learning
And the courage in my heart
With famous beside
I keep growing forward
In grateful light

The Monster

The light flickers on
Growing bright and dim in the same stroke
No clear reason
Other than the past
Leaving the light on too long
Waiting for relief
Relief that never came
Trying to understand the change
Knowing the light keeps holding on
Some days stronger than others
Knowing there is strength
Even when the darkness creeps in
Knowing the monster thrives in the dark
But trying to keep the light on
Sometimes a new place, a new angle, a new
setting
Anything to keep the monster out
Yet the light is dull
Waiting for the surge
That has been seen
But never lasts long
Now waiting the lasting surge
To get the spark
To the brightest of brights
To destroy the monster
That hides so well

Called Back

It's funny really
How old habits kick in
Willing me to be silenced
Stealing any ounce of respect
The hatred creeps in
Invading the power I never had
Willing me to give up
Waiting for me to lie down,
Shut up, close my eyes
And listen to the gentle whisper
Like a siren to a sailor
The voice pulls me to my doom
But I've learned the tricks
I can resist
But sometimes I crumble
Under pressure of perfection
The pain too great
The fear too vast
So the sirens win
But just for the moment
A new day dawns
Before it was ever over
So I swim back to shore
No room to fault
Upon dry land
I can start again

Parasite

The parasite feeds
One day at a time
Stealing the life of an innocent host
Growing more numb to pain
Wishing one pull would take it away
But the parasite clings
Latching on without cease
Never letting up
And infecting with disease
One you cannot see
But slowly destroys the host
Gaining power from pain
Each scream, the next jolt
Jolt of power
For the parasite to grow
As people work to remove
The pain from the host
New people to pull
Sometimes with success
But nothing completely removed
Until my mind finds rest
In strength the parasite will fall
In rest all the pain dissolved
For now the grip holds strong
Feeding on time

Loving the feast
That self doubt provides
But it will disappear
One day removed
Until then, growing
Waiting to renew

Failure

Failure
Failure at recovering
Failure at being sick
Both scary
But one deadly
I never realized the fear
The fear of failing one more person
Even if that person is stealing my life
I have a choice
One I never realized
Save me
Or save ED
Never believing I deserved to be saved
Until I realized I could be
To be saved
I have to choose me
Choose to give myself life
And see my worth
But I don't
Not yet
But I want to
I want the choice to be me
I want to define my worth
See that love I have for others
Given to me

So who will I fail
The girl I am
or the monster inside
I know my choice
But will I be able to decide

Free

Every journey unique
Every experience ones own
Not how we planned
But a chance to learn and grow
Failure met by growth
Changing from failure to learning
No right way
No straight path
But eyes set ahead
To a life set free
Free from the shame that grips
Free from pain
Free from the steps that lead closer to emptiness
There is no one clear way
Because life is a gift
That changes every day
Interpreted by the beholder
So look at the blank pages in your life
Write them with tenacity
In the unknown keep going
Turn the page
Change the narrative of your view
Not to ignore the story
But to keep it going
The story doesn't have to end

The story may be hard
But if it wasn't hard how would we learn
Every time we stumble
Stand tall
Even when we stumble back
Don't stay down
You are loved
You are strong
Keep your story going
Because your story is worth it

The Army

You changed my view
You helped me see
What I just couldn't seem to believe
See that I was worth it
See that I deserved to heal
Although I still battle
I do not fear
I have the tools
I have the support
To keep moving forward
Even in the dark
I may not know the end
I may not see the path
But I'm never alone on this earth
I know I'm loved
Even when I don't believe
I breathe in the good
And exhale the doubt
Everyday a new battle abounds
But I'm strengthened in God
I'm strengthened with you
My entire army
I never even knew
Knew I needed
Or knew how you would help

But you made a difference
You helped me out
Out of the darkest days
That I have no doubt

Chapter 2

The hard steps being taken
The pages being turned
The journey long
But there is joy in how far I've come
The mind far from silent
But no longer alone
The hard words spoken
The race being run
I never imagined this path
One that has made me stronger
Has made me see
Has made me wonder
But I know for sure
I have this fight
Because even if I stumble
I will find the light
So now it's time
To turn the next page
To keep on running
And see the next race
One that I know
But have clearer eyes to see
I will beat ED
I will be free
Free in mind

Free in body
Free in spirit
Now I have a full army
One where I can lead the charge
So here is to chapter 2
The next stage of growth
Hard, but I know I can do this too

www.ingramcontent.com/pod-product-compliance
Lightning Source LLC
La Vergne TN
LVHW010920200726
843509LV00013B/2008

9789357616997